GRAPHIC LIBRARY™

DISASTERS IN HISTORY

THE GREAT CHICAGO FIRE OF 1871

by Kay Melchisedech Olson

illustrated by Phil Miller and
Charles Barnett III

Consultant:

Richard F. Bales, author

*The Great Chicago Fire and the
Myth of Mrs. O'Leary's Cow*

Capstone

Mankato, Minnesota

Graphic Library is published by Capstone Press,
1710 Roe Crest Drive, North Mankato, Minnesota 56003.
www.capstonepub.com

Printed in the United States of America in Stevens Point, Wisconsin.

052016
009764R

Books published by Capstone Press are manufactured with paper containing at least 10 percent post-consumer waste.

Library of Congress Cataloging-in-Publication Data
Olson, Kay Melchisedech.
The Great Chicago Fire of 1871 / by Kay M. Olson; illustrated by Phil Miller and Charles Barnett III.
p. cm.—(Graphic library. Disasters in history)
Includes bibliographical references and index.
ISBN-13: 978-0-7368-5480-1 (hardcover)
ISBN-10: 0-7368-5480-0 (hardcover)
ISBN-13: 978-0-7368-6875-4 (softcover pbk.)
ISBN-10: 0-7368-6875-5 (softcover pbk.)
1. Great Fire, Chicago, Ill., 1871—Juvenile literature. 2. Fires—Illinois—Chicago—History—19th century—Juvenile literature. 3. Chicago (Ill.)—History—To 1875—Juvenile literature. I. Miller, Phil, ill. II. Barnett, Charles, III, ill. III. Title. IV. Series.
F548.42.O47 2006
977.3'11041—dc22 2005029861

Summmary: In graphic novel format, tells the story of the Great Chicago Fire of 1871, an inferno that forever changed the city's skyline.

Art Direction and Design
Bob Lentz

Storyboard and Production Artist
Alison Thiele

Colorist
Matt Webb

Editor
Donald Lemke

TABLE OF CONTENTS

CHAPTER 1
FIRST FLAMES

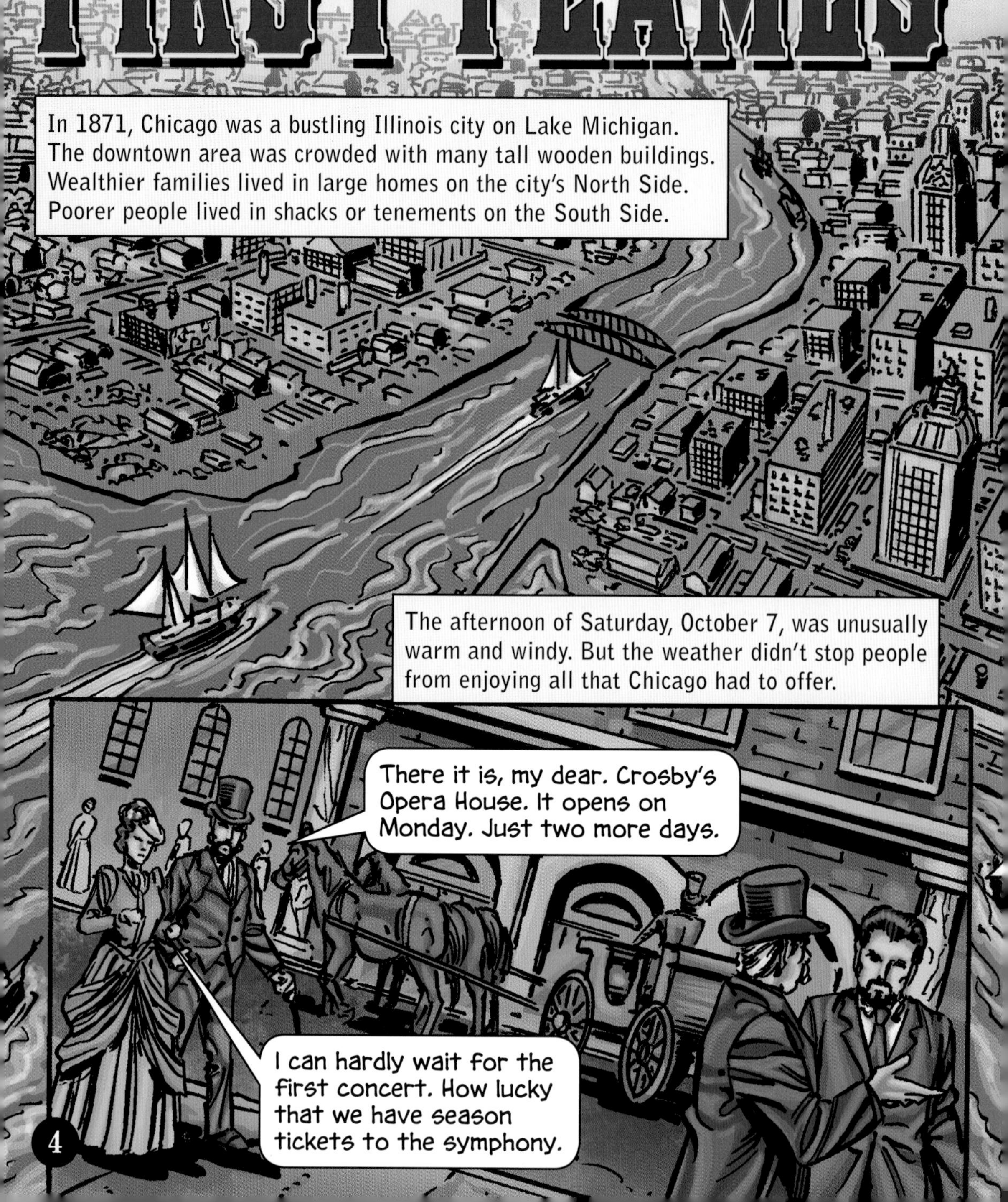
In 1871, Chicago was a bustling Illinois city on Lake Michigan. The downtown area was crowded with many tall wooden buildings. Wealthier families lived in large homes on the city's North Side. Poorer people lived in shacks or tenements on the South Side.
The afternoon of Saturday, October 7, was unusually warm and windy. But the weather didn't stop people from enjoying all that Chicago had to offer.
There it is, my dear. Crosby's Opera House. It opens on Monday. Just two more days.
I can hardly wait for the first concert. How lucky that we have season tickets to the symphony.

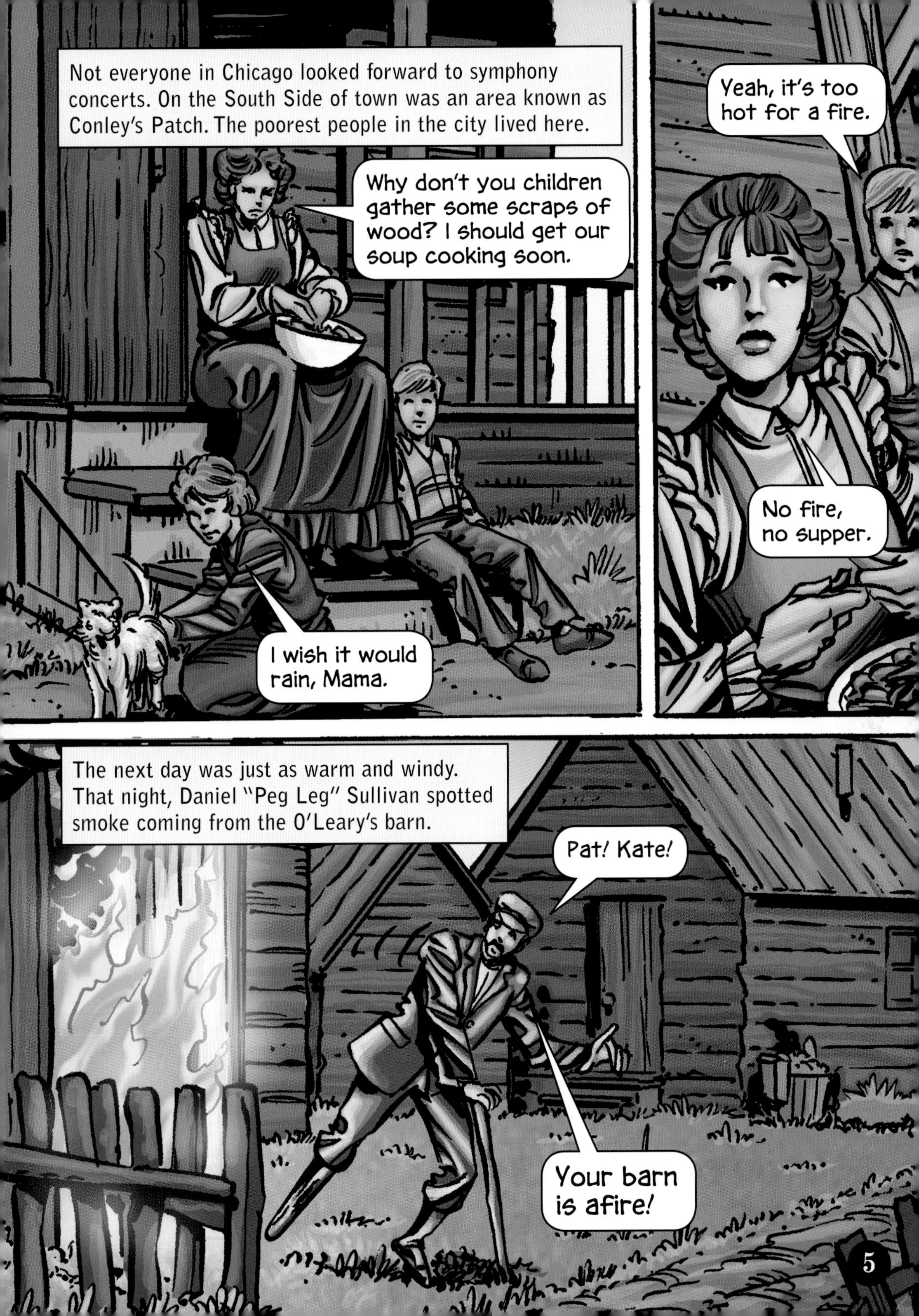

Not everyone in Chicago looked forward to symphony concerts. On the South Side of town was an area known as Conley's Patch. The poorest people in the city lived here.
Why don't you children gather some scraps of wood? I should get our soup cooking soon.
I wish it would rain, Mama.
Yeah, it's too hot for a fire.
No fire, no supper.
The next day was just as warm and windy. That night, Daniel "Peg Leg" Sullivan spotted smoke coming from the O'Leary's barn.
Pat! Kate!
Your barn is afire!

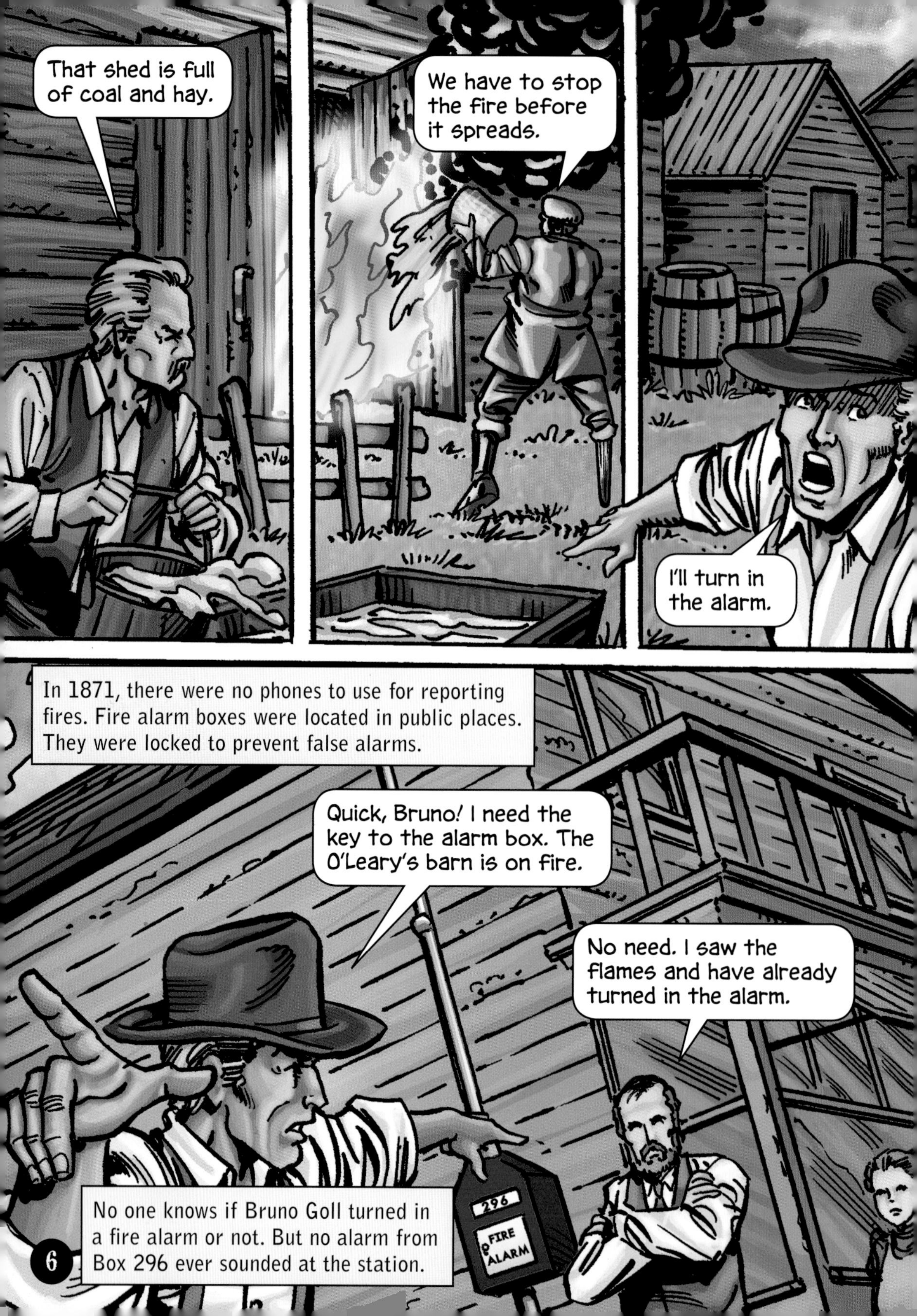
That shed is full of coal and hay.
We have to stop the fire before it spreads.
I'll turn in the alarm.
In 1871, there were no phones to use for reporting fires. Fire alarm boxes were located in public places. They were locked to prevent false alarms.
Quick, Bruno! I need the key to the alarm box. The O'Leary's barn is on fire.
No need. I saw the flames and have already turned in the alarm.
296
FIRE ALARM
No one knows if Bruno Goll turned in a fire alarm or not. But no alarm from Box 296 ever sounded at the station.

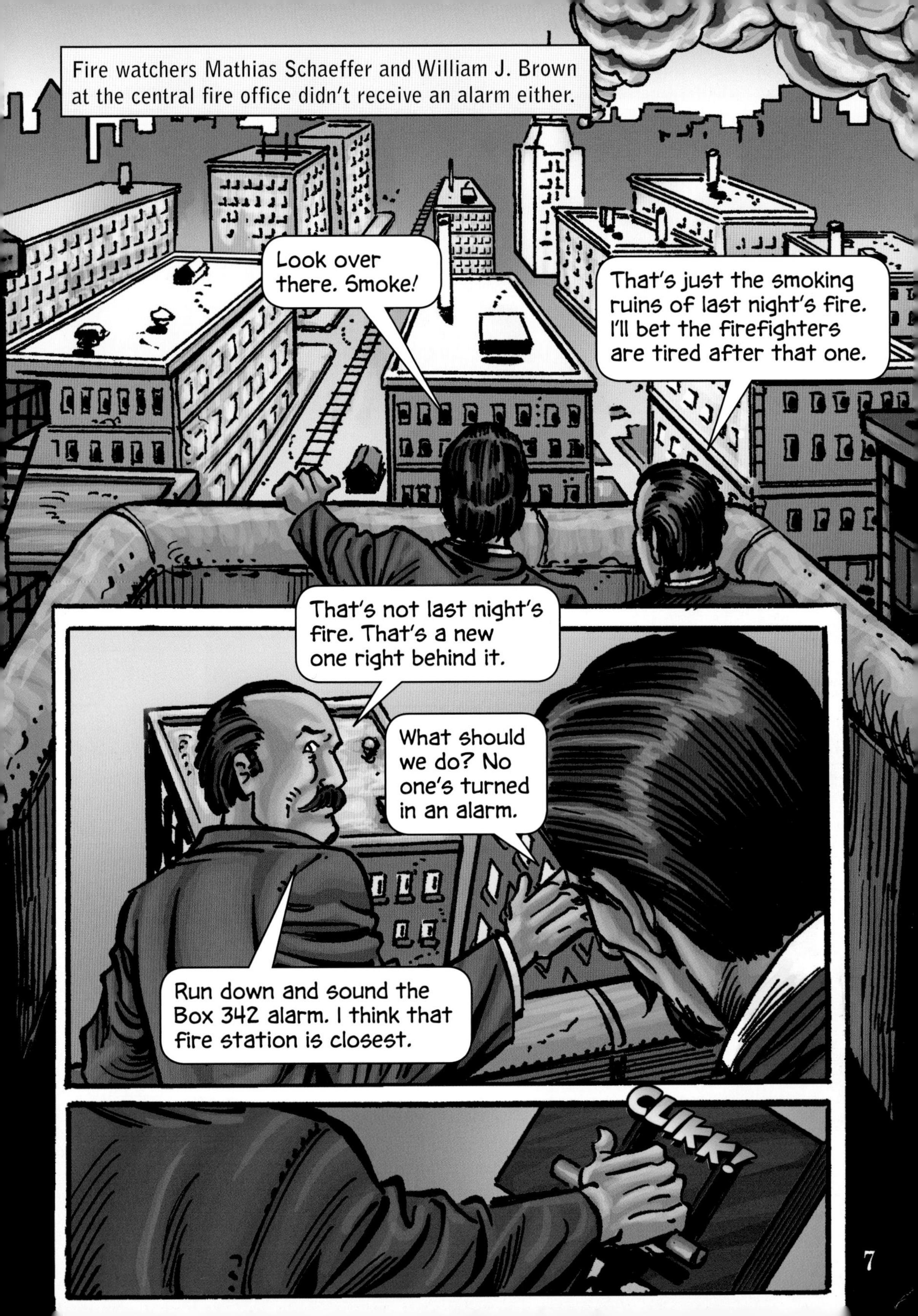
Fire watchers Mathias Schaeffer and William J. Brown at the central fire office didn't receive an alarm either.
Look over there. Smoke!
That's just the smoking ruins of last night's fire. I'll bet the firefighters are tired after that one.
That's not last night's fire. That's a new one right behind it.
What should we do? No one's turned in an alarm.
Run down and sound the Box 342 alarm. I think that fire station is closest.
CLIKK!

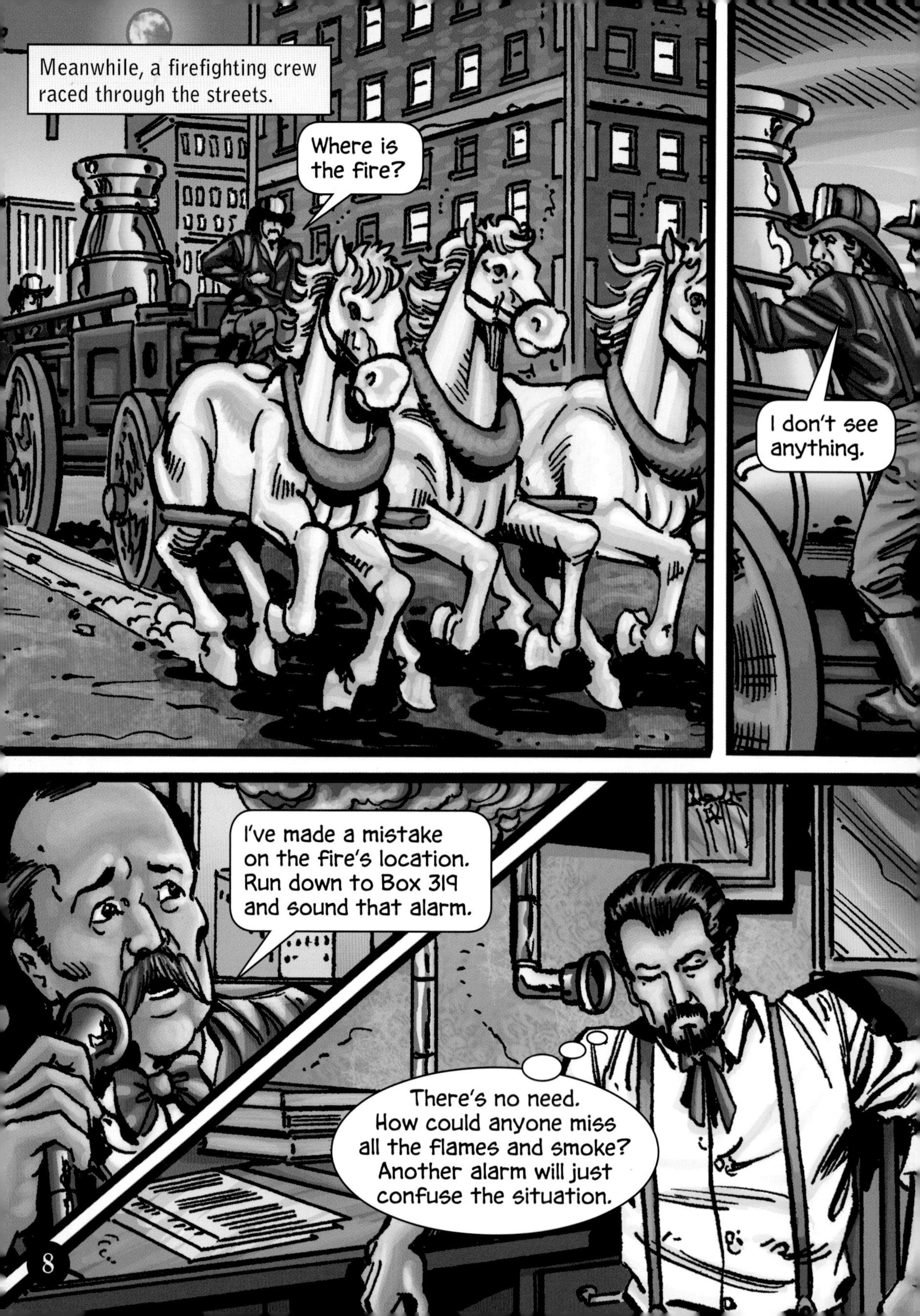
Meanwhile, a firefighting crew raced through the streets.
Where is the fire?
I don't see anything.
I've made a mistake on the fire's location. Run down to Box 319 and sound that alarm.
There's no need. How could anyone miss all the flames and smoke? Another alarm will just confuse the situation.

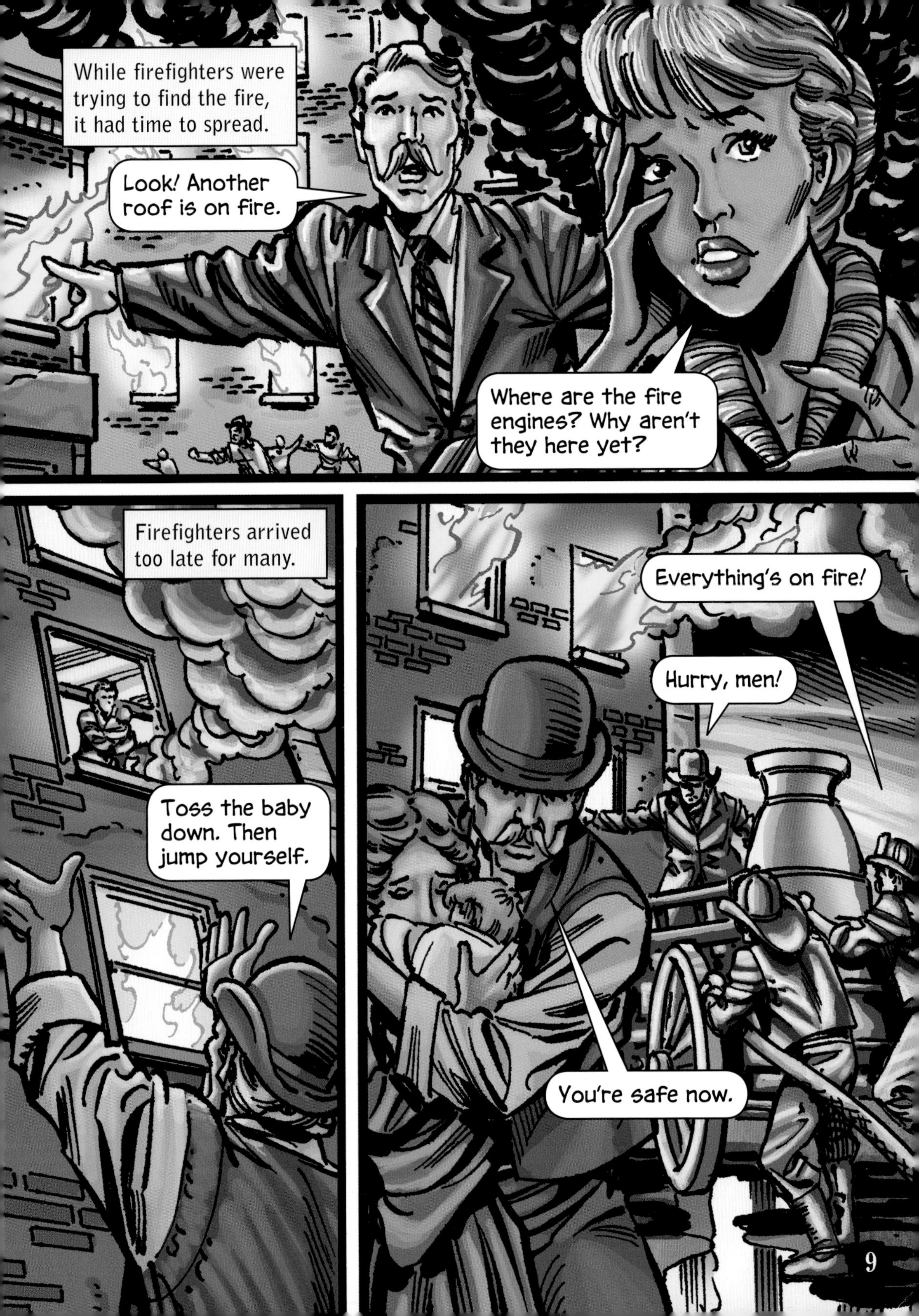
While firefighters were trying to find the fire, it had time to spread.
Look! Another roof is on fire.
Where are the fire engines? Why aren't they here yet?
Firefighters arrived too late for many.
Toss the baby down. Then jump yourself.
Everything's on fire!
Hurry, men!
You're safe now.

CHAPTER 2
GROWING PANIC

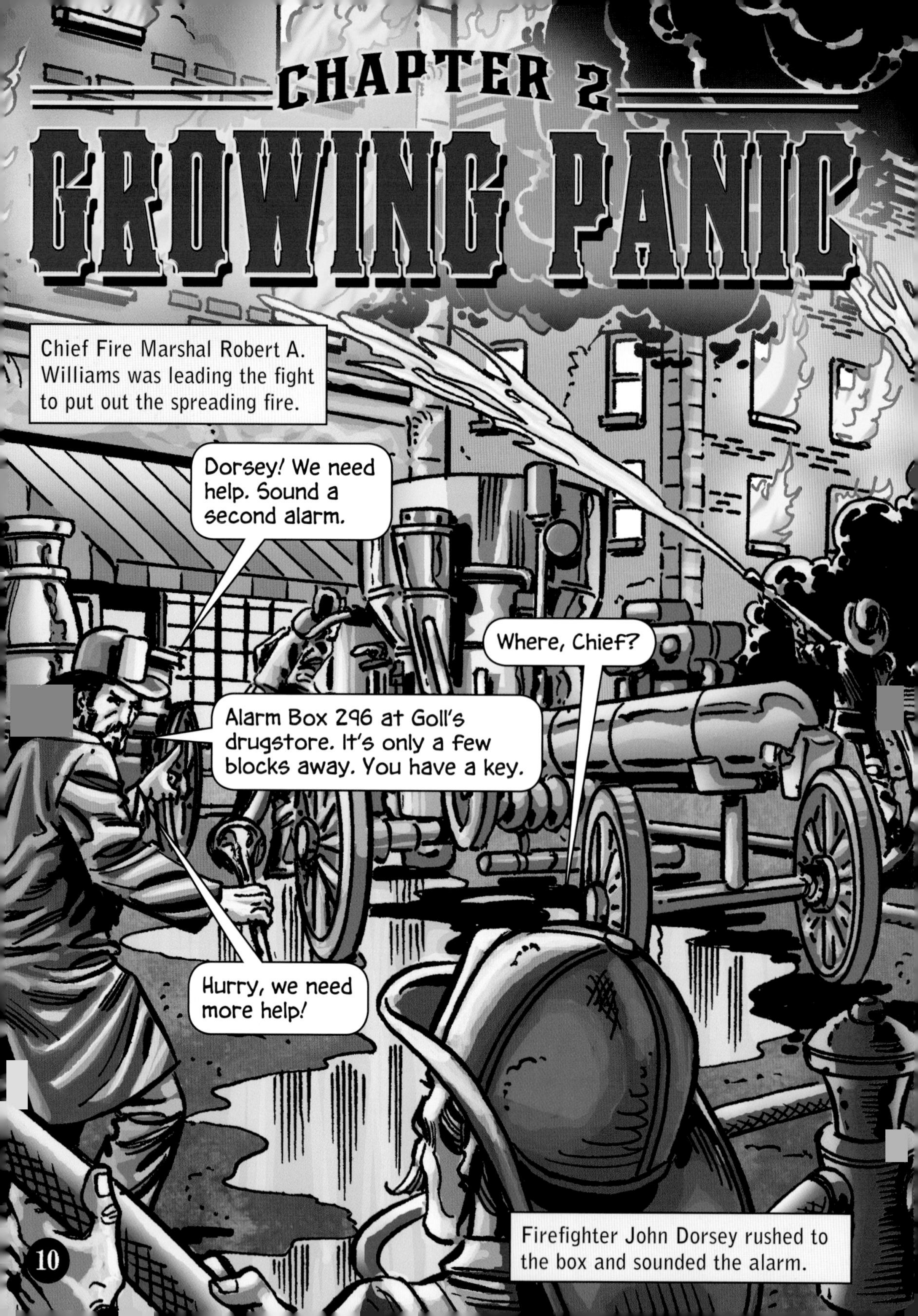
Chief Fire Marshal Robert A. Williams was leading the fight to put out the spreading fire.
Dorsey! We need help. Sound a second alarm.
Where, Chief?
Alarm Box 296 at Goll's drugstore. It's only a few blocks away. You have a key.
Hurry, we need more help!
Firefighter John Dorsey rushed to the box and sounded the alarm.

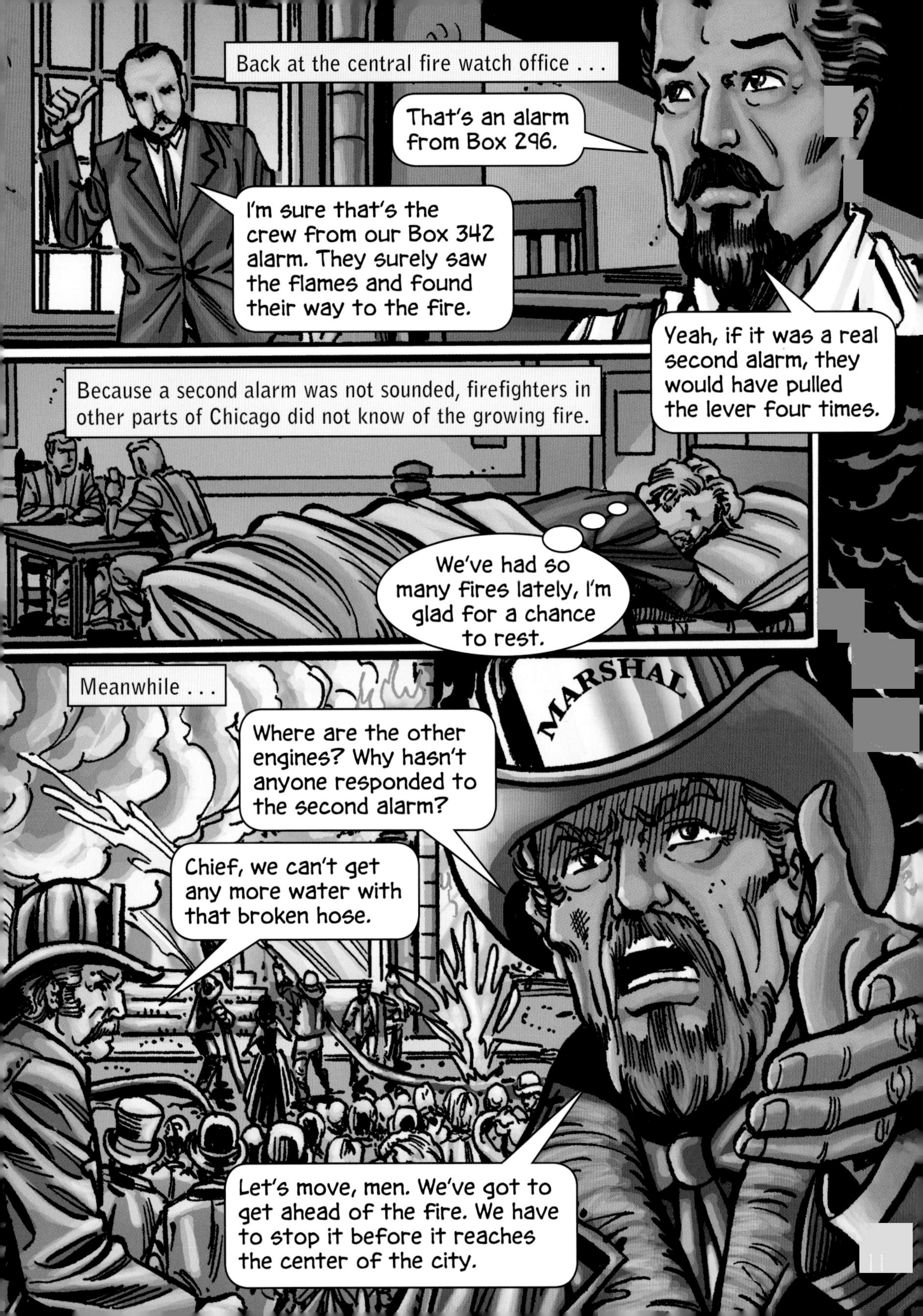
Back at the central fire watch office . . .
That's an alarm from Box 296.
I'm sure that's the crew from our Box 342 alarm. They surely saw the flames and found their way to the fire.
Yeah, if it was a real second alarm, they would have pulled the lever four times.
Because a second alarm was not sounded, firefighters in other parts of Chicago did not know of the growing fire.
We've had so many fires lately, I'm glad for a chance to rest.
Meanwhile . . .
MARSHAL
Where are the other engines? Why hasn't anyone responded to the second alarm?
Chief, we can't get any more water with that broken hose.
Let's move, men. We've got to get ahead of the fire. We have to stop it before it reaches the center of the city.

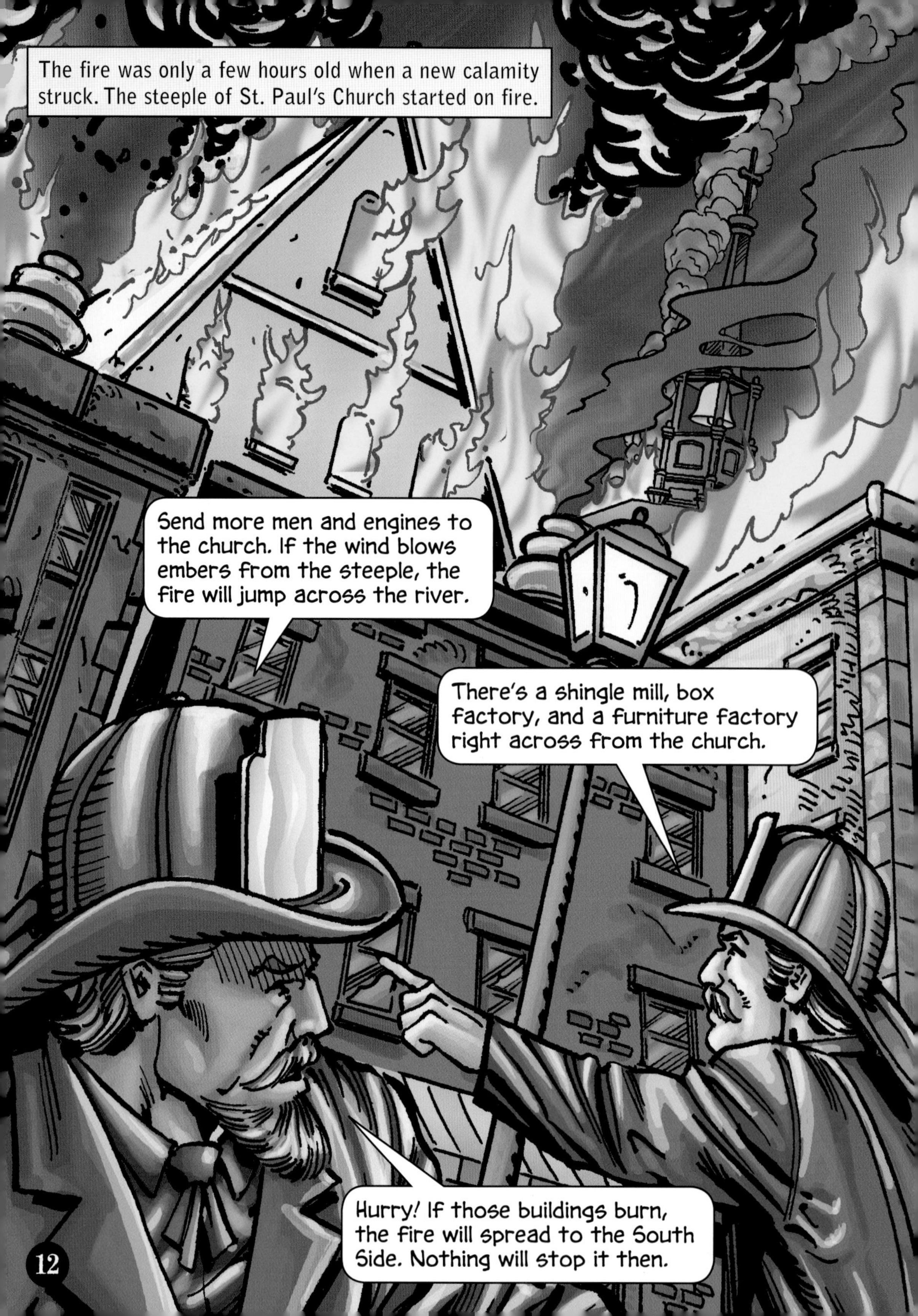
The fire was only a few hours old when a new calamity struck. The steeple of St. Paul's Church started on fire.
Send more men and engines to the church. If the wind blows embers from the steeple, the fire will jump across the river.
There's a shingle mill, box factory, and a furniture factory right across from the church.
Hurry! If those buildings burn, the fire will spread to the South Side. Nothing will stop it then.

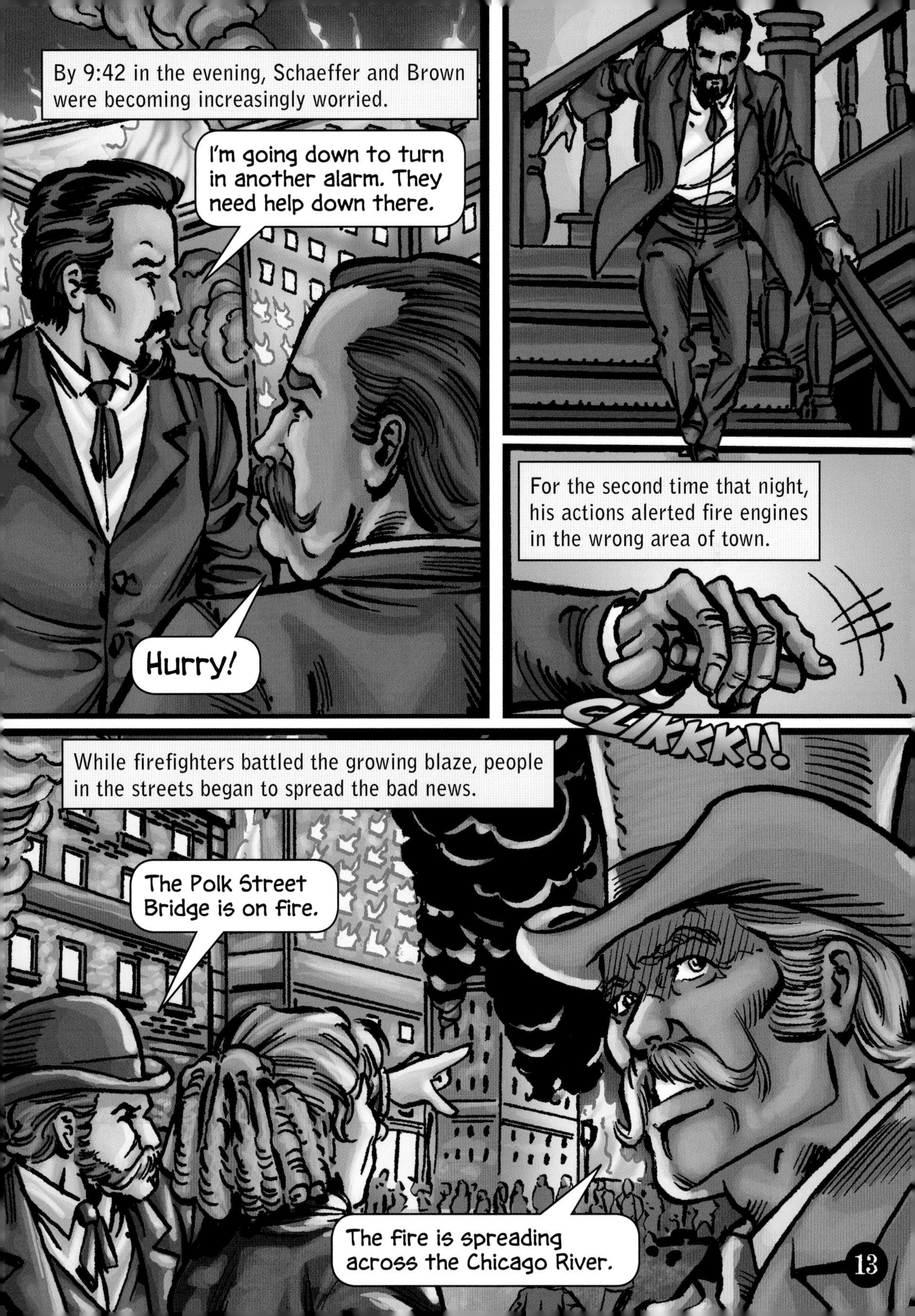
By 9:42 in the evening, Schaeffer and Brown were becoming increasingly worried.
I'm going down to turn in another alarm. They need help down there.
Hurry!
For the second time that night, his actions alerted fire engines in the wrong area of town.
CLIKKK!!
While firefighters battled the growing blaze, people in the streets began to spread the bad news.
The Polk Street Bridge is on fire.
The fire is spreading across the Chicago River.

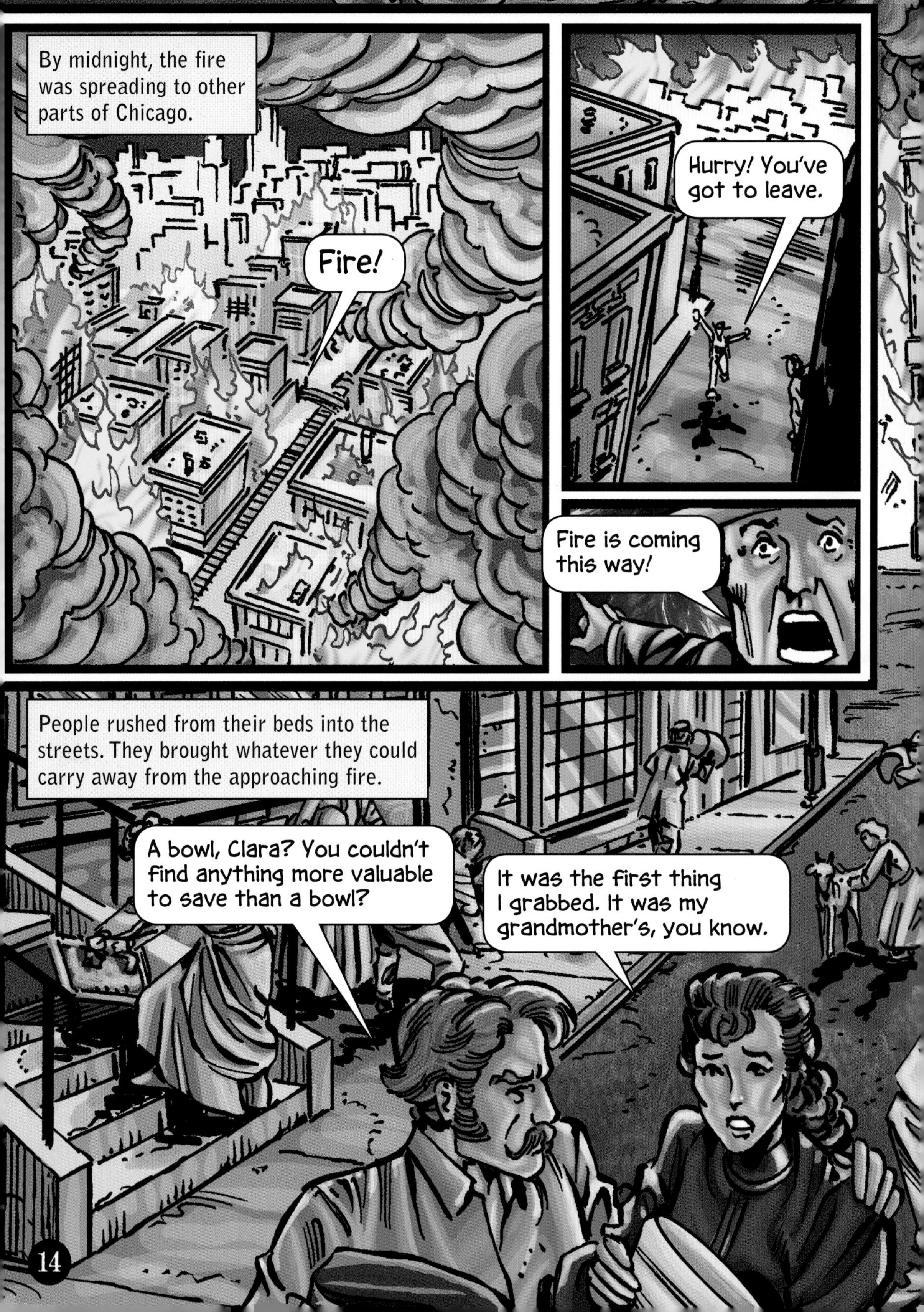
By midnight, the fire was spreading to other parts of Chicago.
Fire!
Hurry! You've got to leave.
Fire is coming this way!
People rushed from their beds into the streets. They brought whatever they could carry away from the approaching fire.
A bowl, Clara? You couldn't find anything more valuable to save than a bowl?
It was the first thing I grabbed. It was my grandmother's, you know.

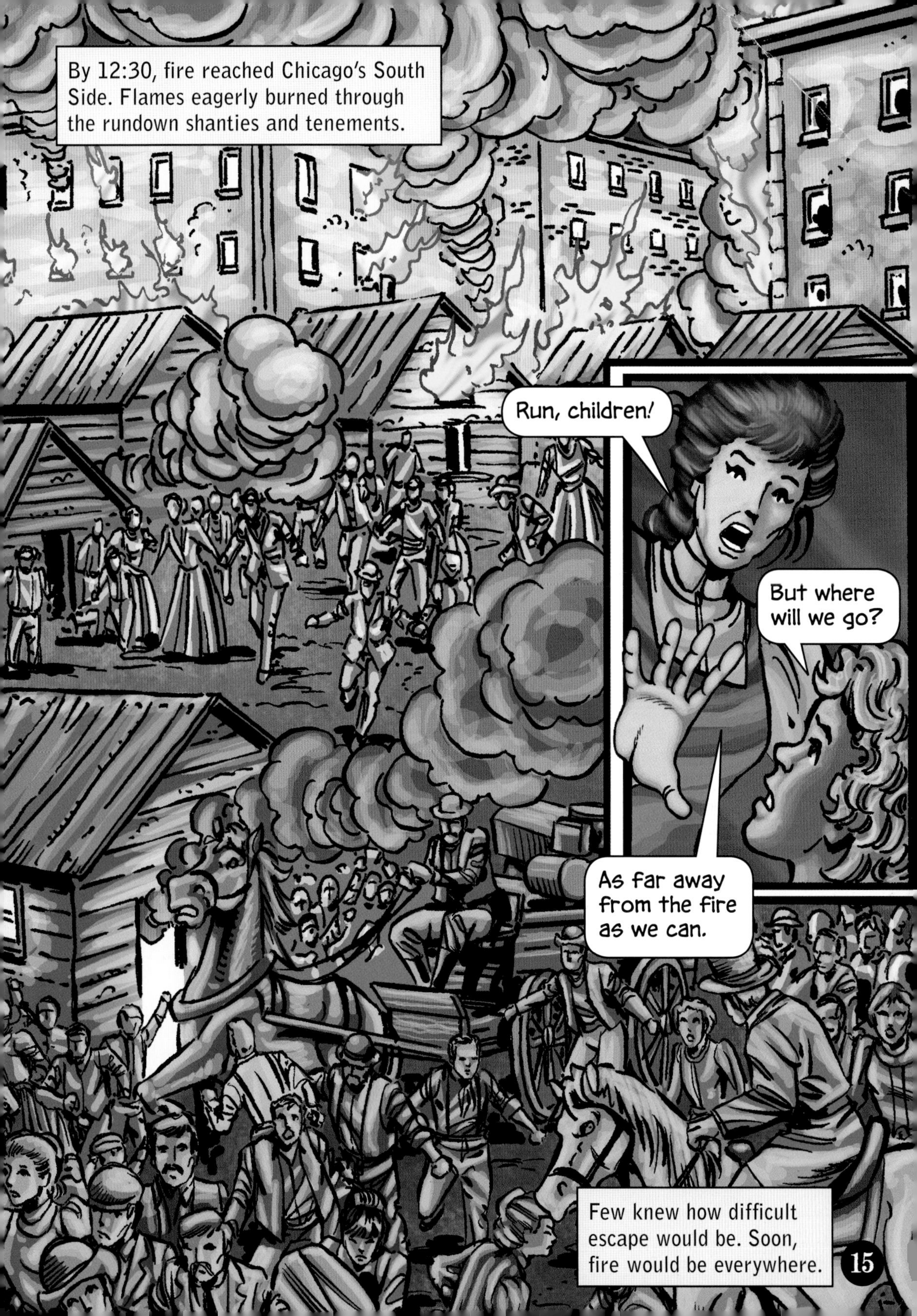
By 12:30, fire reached Chicago's South Side. Flames eagerly burned through the rundown shanties and tenements.
Run, children!
But where will we go?
As far away from the fire as we can.
Few knew how difficult escape would be. Soon, fire would be everywhere.

CHAPTER 3
TOTAL DISASTER

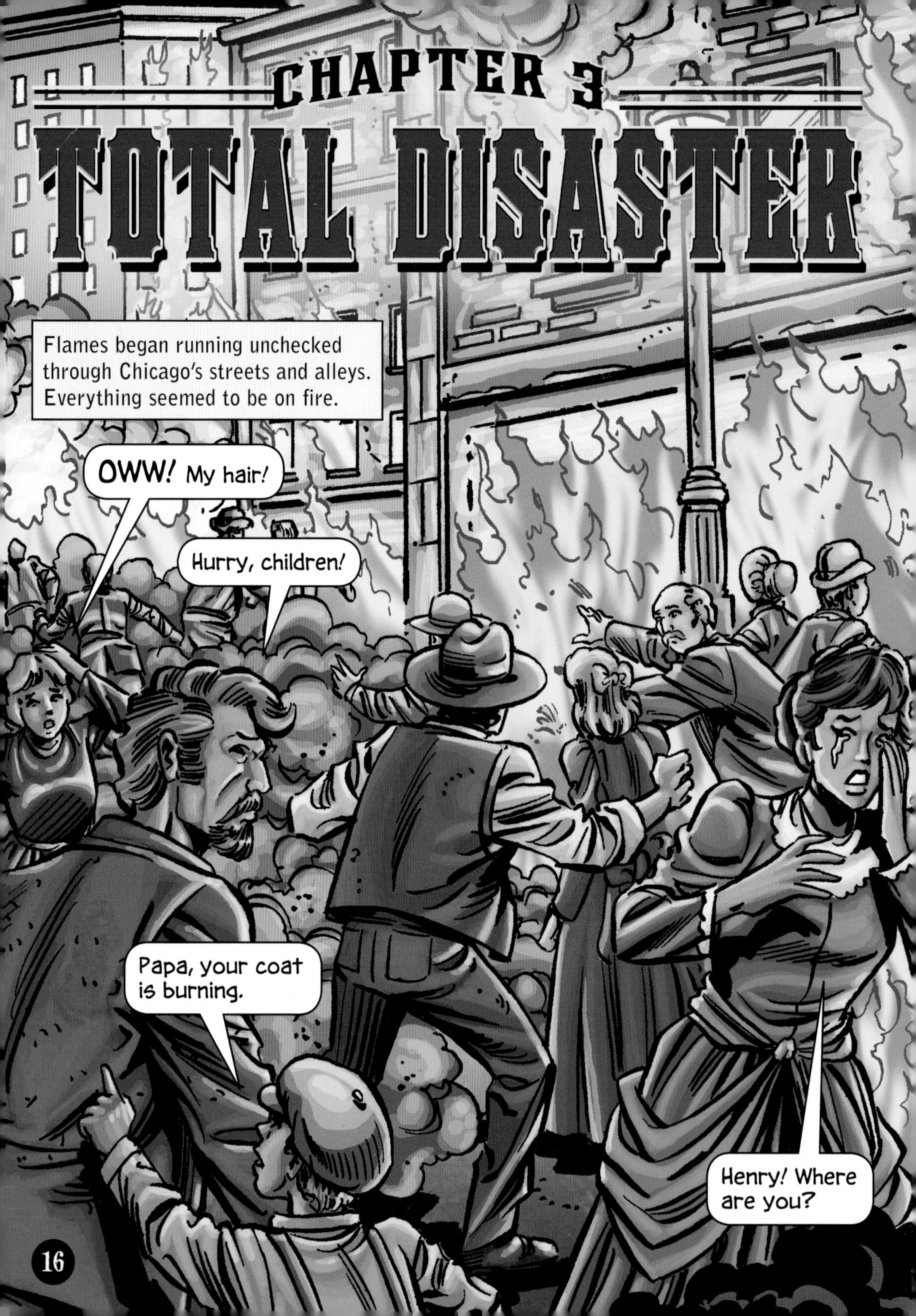

Flames began running unchecked through Chicago's streets and alleys. Everything seemed to be on fire.
OWW! My hair!
Hurry, children!
Papa, your coat is burning.
Henry! Where are you?

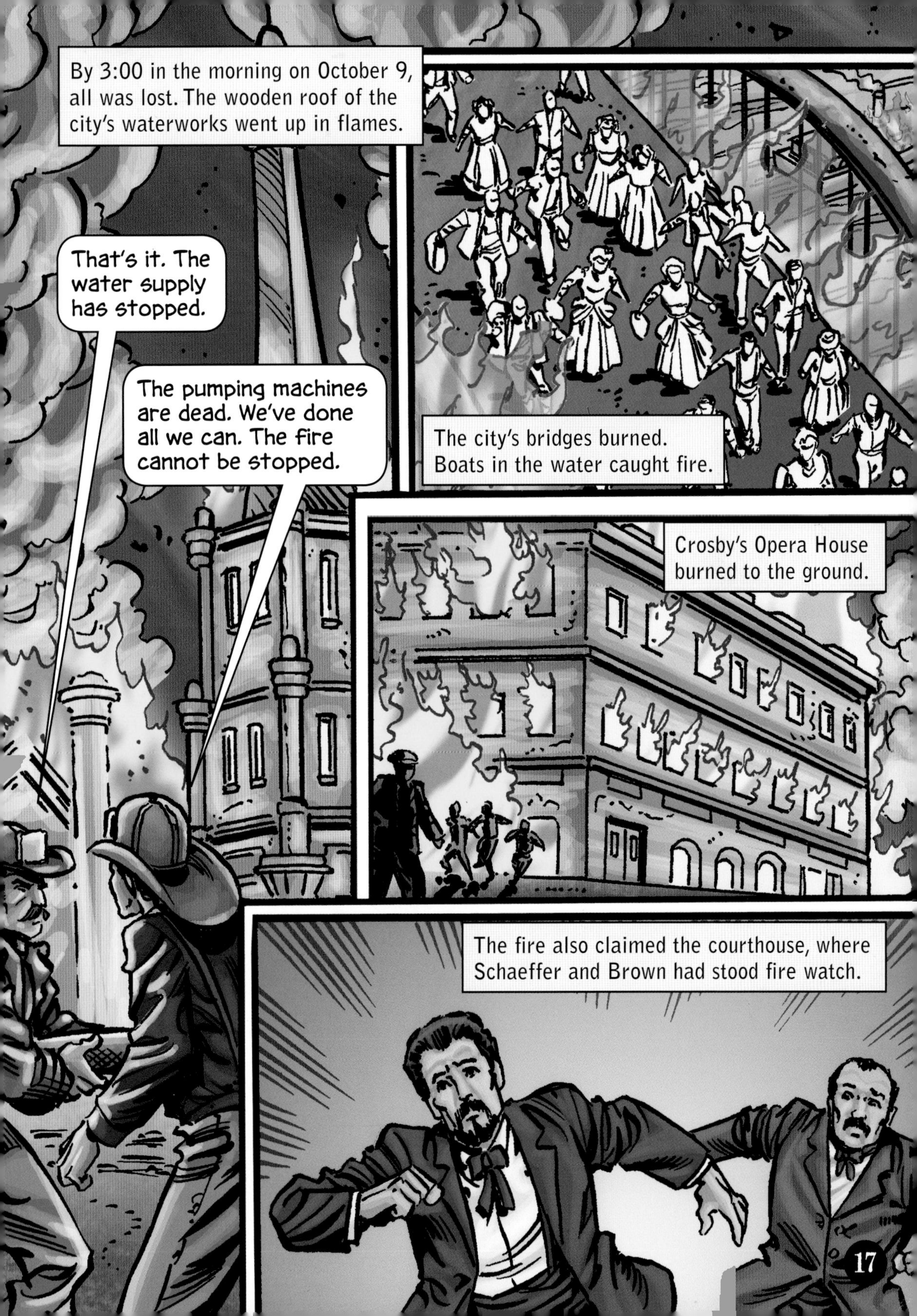
By 3:00 in the morning on October 9, all was lost. The wooden roof of the city's waterworks went up in flames.
That's it. The water supply has stopped.
The pumping machines are dead. We've done all we can. The fire cannot be stopped.
The city's bridges burned. Boats in the water caught fire.
Crosby's Opera House burned to the ground.
The fire also claimed the courthouse, where Schaeffer and Brown had stood fire watch.

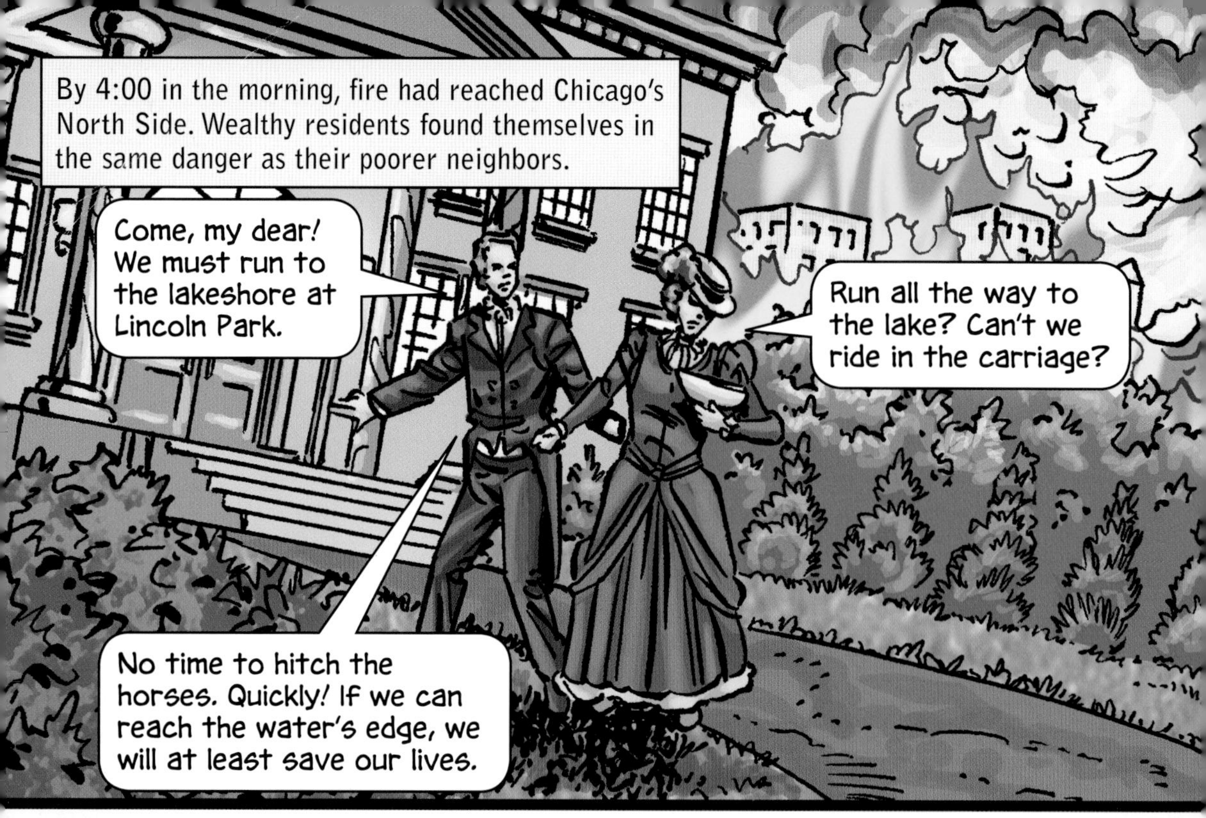
By 4:00 in the morning, fire had reached Chicago's North Side. Wealthy residents found themselves in the same danger as their poorer neighbors.
Come, my dear! We must run to the lakeshore at Lincoln Park.
Run all the way to the lake? Can't we ride in the carriage?
No time to hitch the horses. Quickly! If we can reach the water's edge, we will at least save our lives.

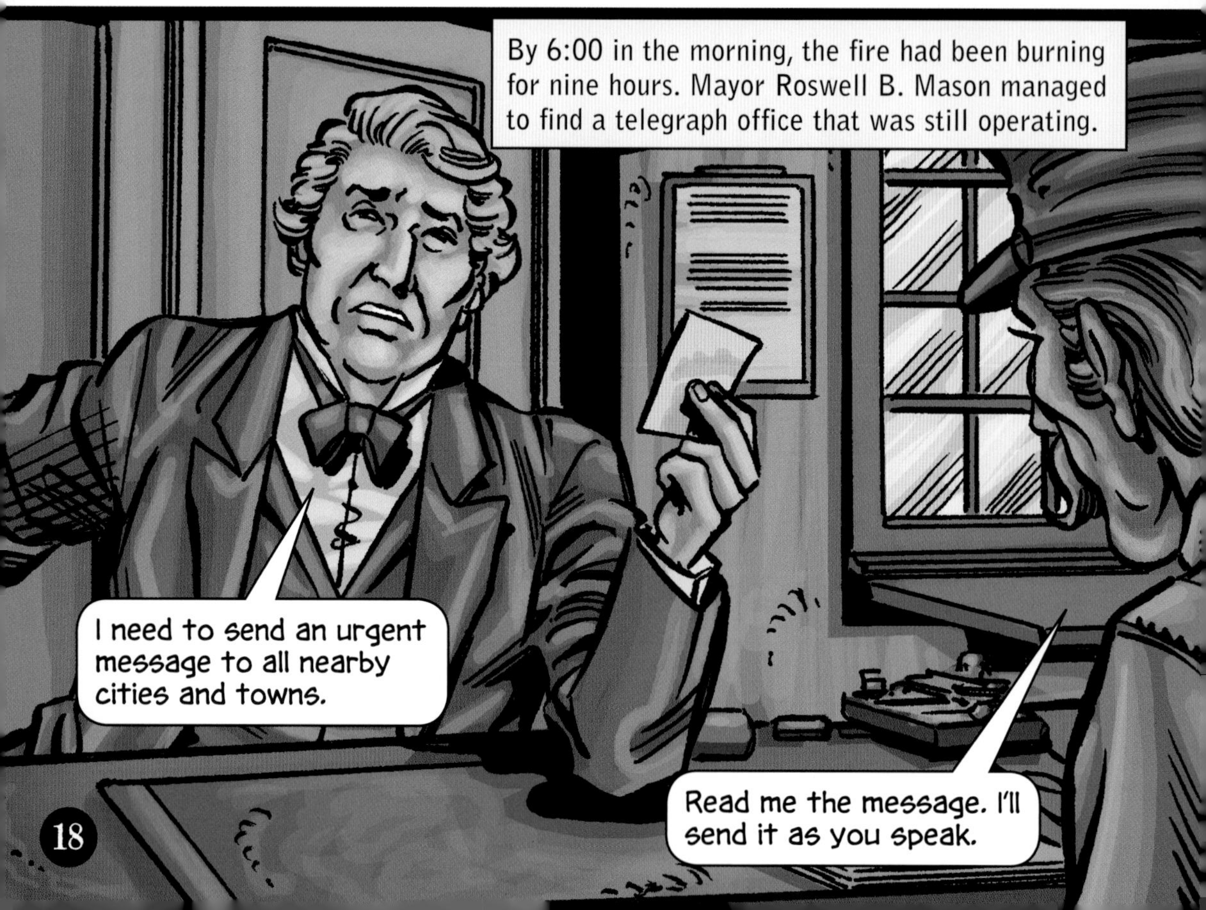
By 6:00 in the morning, the fire had been burning for nine hours. Mayor Roswell B. Mason managed to find a telegraph office that was still operating.
I need to send an urgent message to all nearby cities and towns.
Read me the message. I'll send it as you speak.

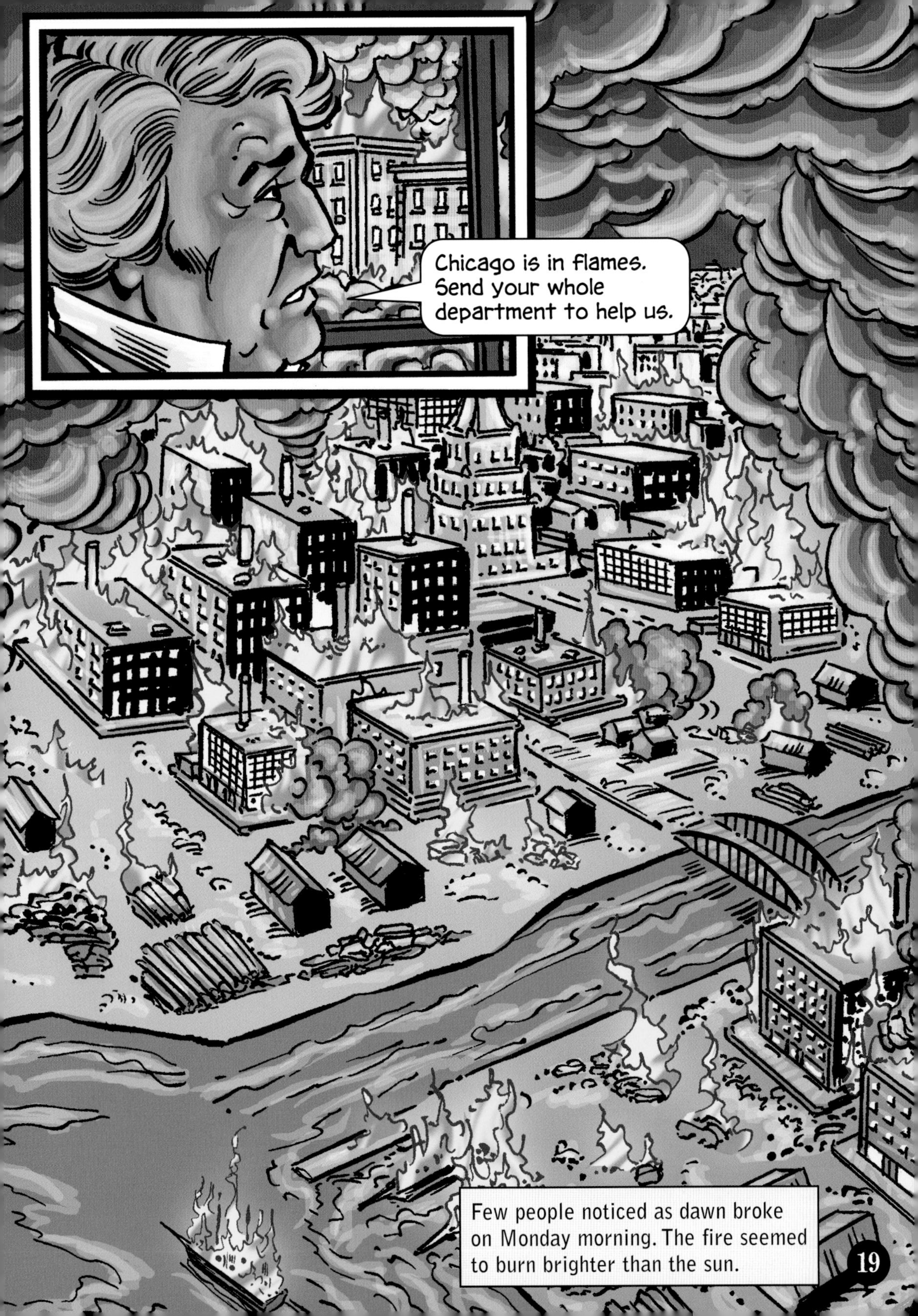
Chicago is in flames. Send your whole department to help us.
Few people noticed as dawn broke on Monday morning. The fire seemed to burn brighter than the sun.

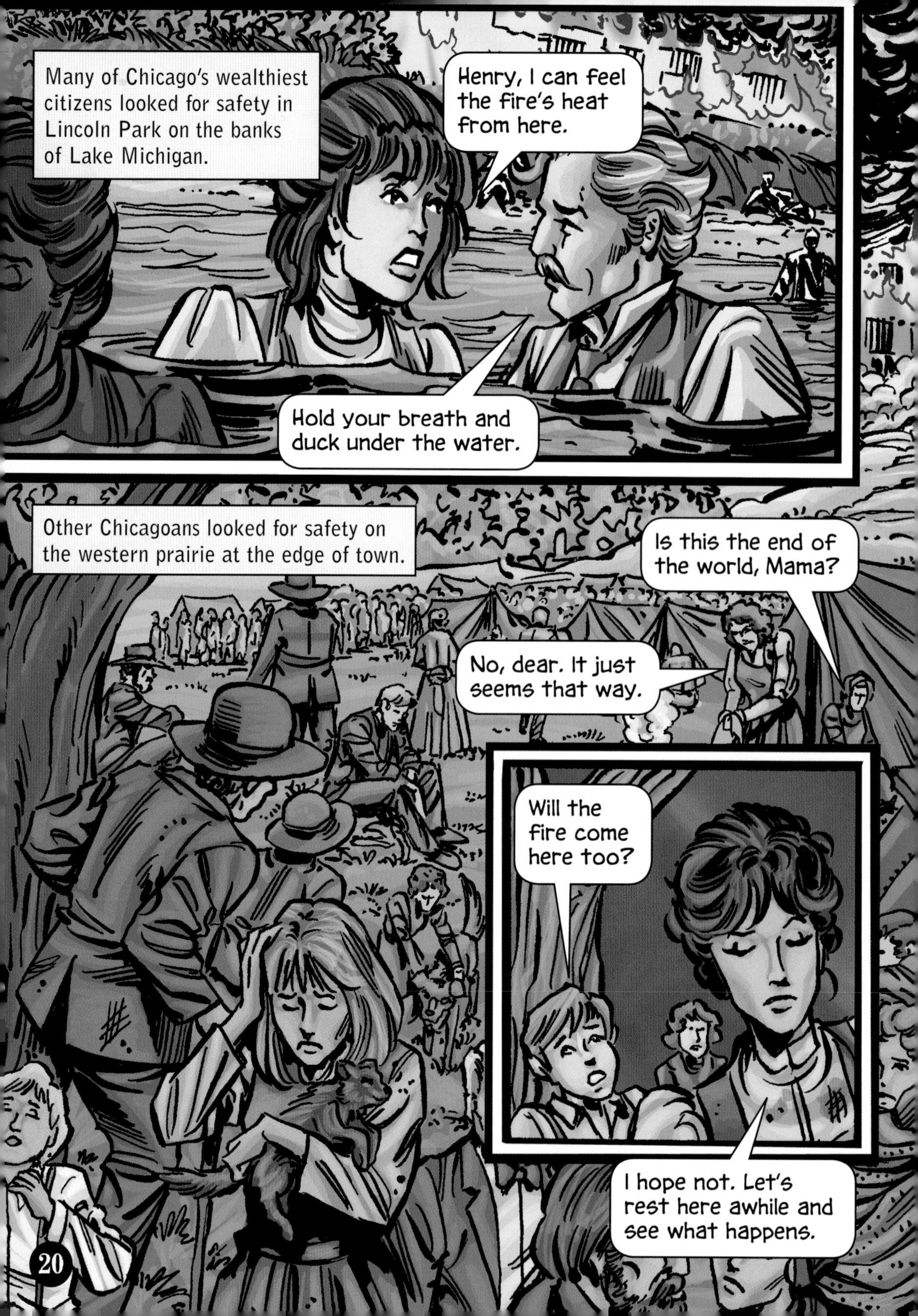

Many of Chicago's wealthiest citizens looked for safety in Lincoln Park on the banks of Lake Michigan.
Henry, I can feel the fire's heat from here.
Hold your breath and duck under the water.
Other Chicagoans looked for safety on the western prairie at the edge of town.
Is this the end of the world, Mama?
No, dear. It just seems that way.
Will the fire come here too?
I hope not. Let's rest here awhile and see what happens.

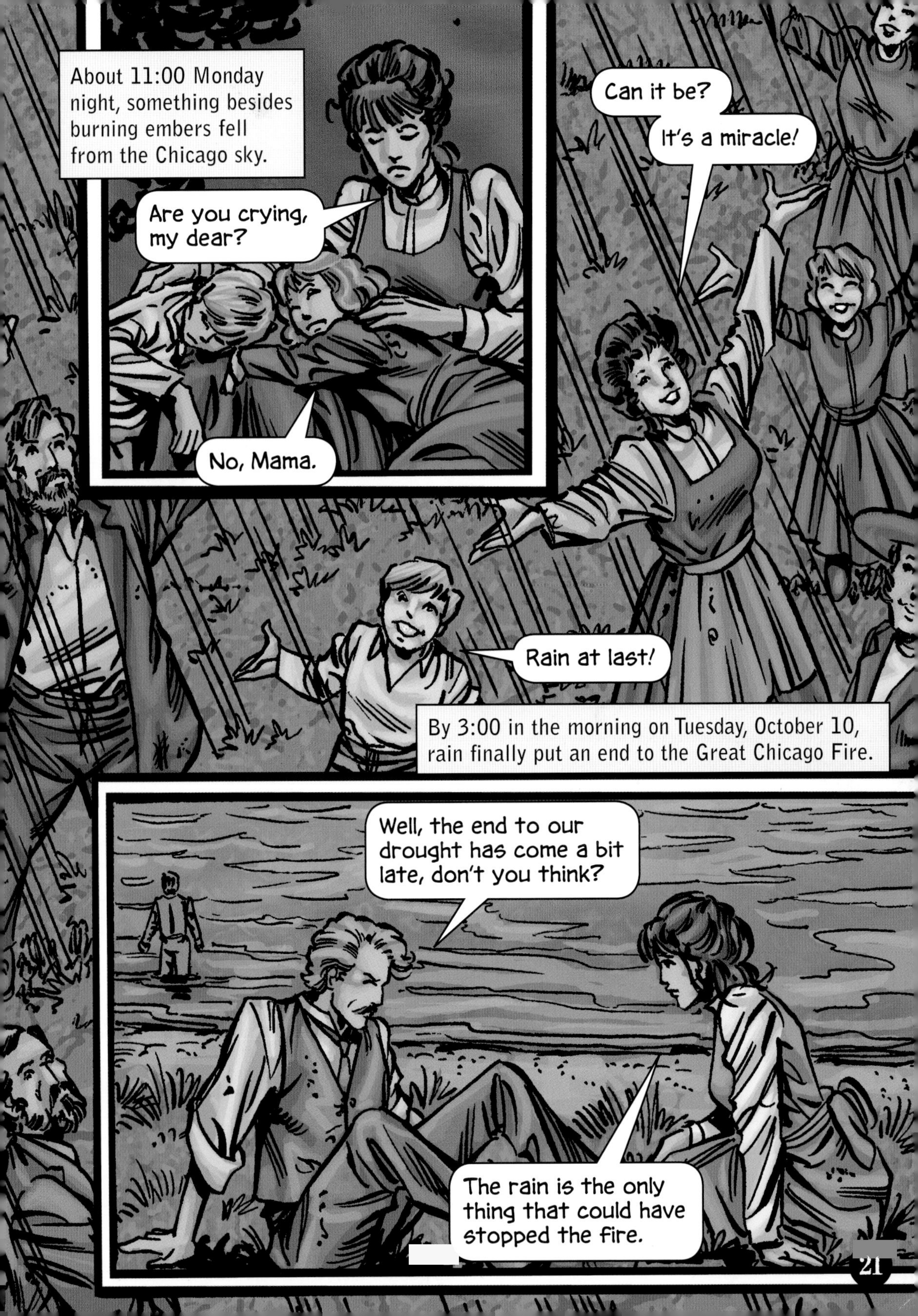

About 11:00 Monday night, something besides burning embers fell from the Chicago sky.
Are you crying, my dear?
No, Mama.
Can it be?
It's a miracle!
Rain at last!
By 3:00 in the morning on Tuesday, October 10, rain finally put an end to the Great Chicago Fire.
Well, the end to our drought has come a bit late, don't you think?
The rain is the only thing that could have stopped the fire.

CHAPTER 4
AFTER THE ASHES

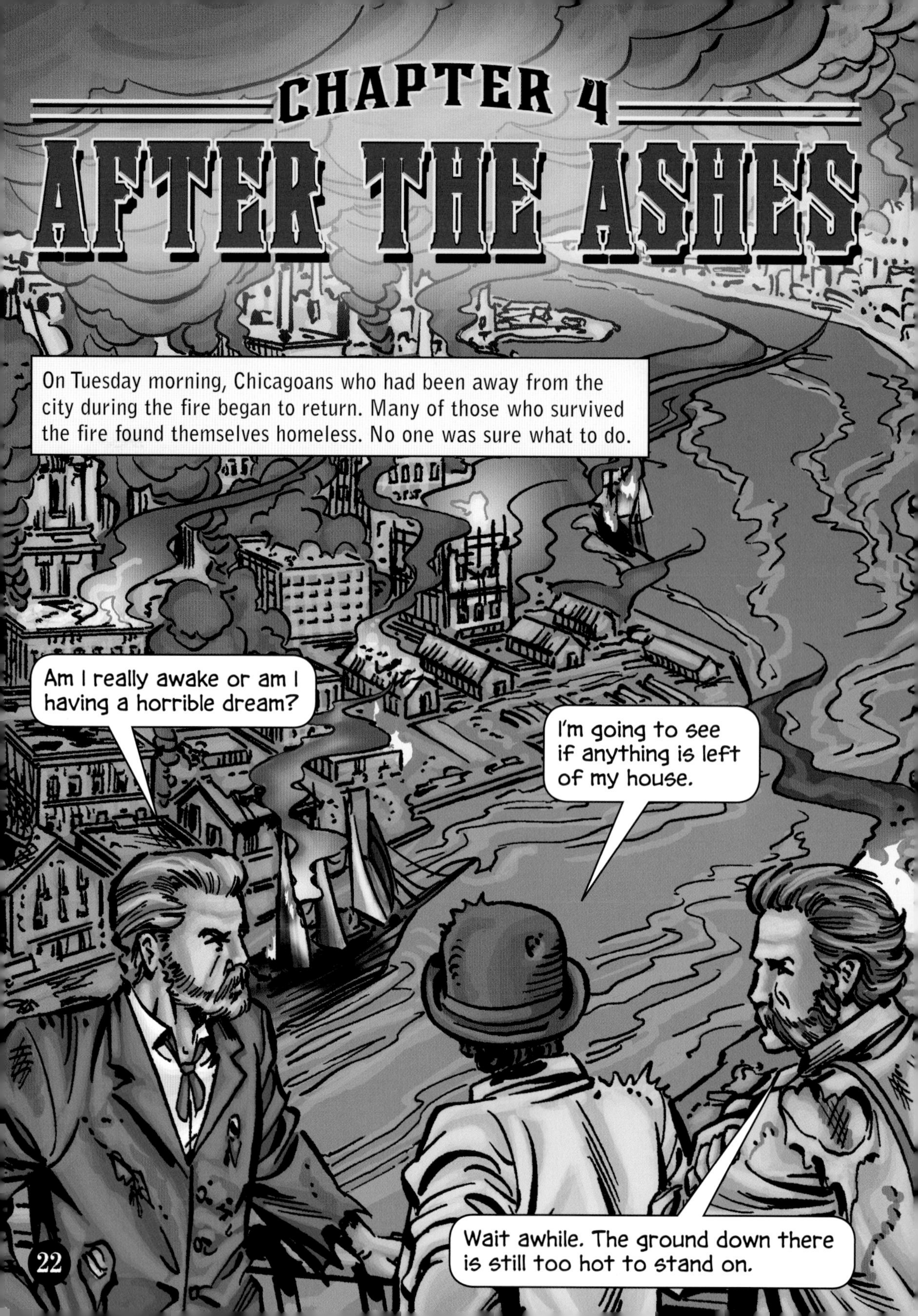
On Tuesday morning, Chicagoans who had been away from the city during the fire began to return. Many of those who survived the fire found themselves homeless. No one was sure what to do.
Am I really awake or am I having a horrible dream?
I'm going to see if anything is left of my house.
Wait awhile. The ground down there is still too hot to stand on.

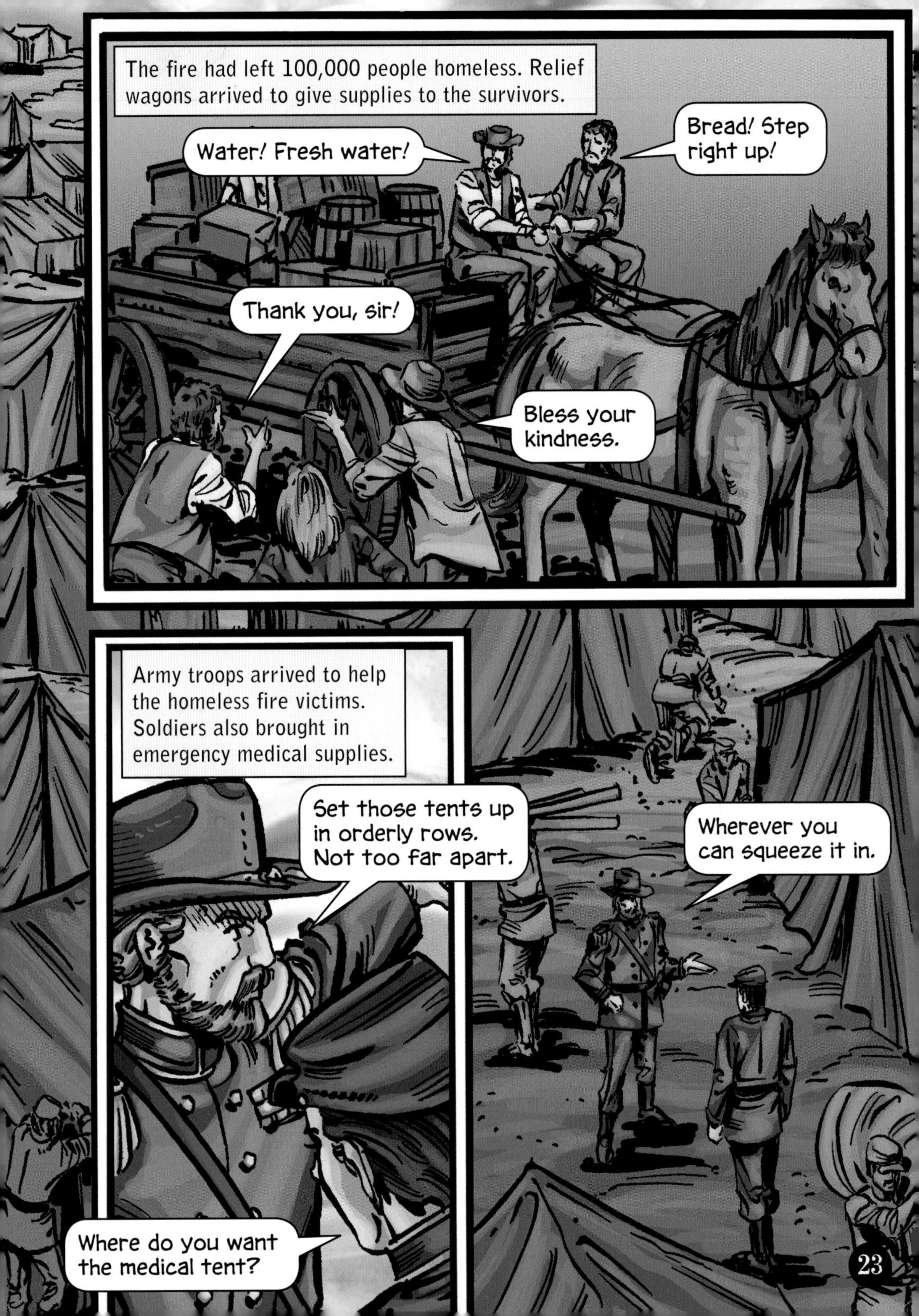

The fire had left 100,000 people homeless. Relief wagons arrived to give supplies to the survivors.
Water! Fresh water!
Bread! Step right up!
Thank you, sir!
Bless your kindness.
Army troops arrived to help the homeless fire victims. Soldiers also brought in emergency medical supplies.
Set those tents up in orderly rows. Not too far apart.
Where do you want the medical tent?
Wherever you can squeeze it in.

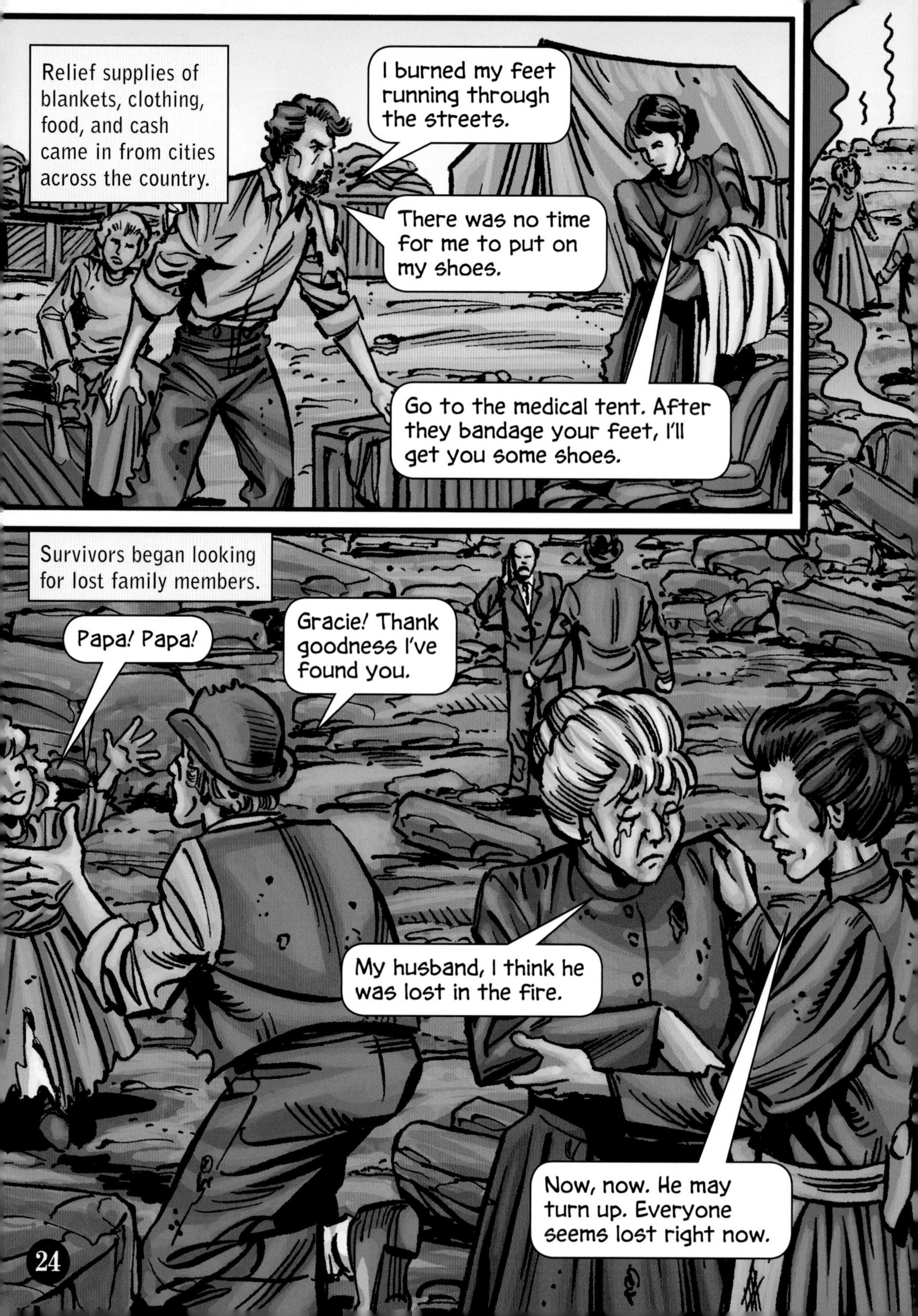
Relief supplies of blankets, clothing, food, and cash came in from cities across the country.
I burned my feet running through the streets.
There was no time for me to put on my shoes.
Go to the medical tent. After they bandage your feet, I'll get you some shoes.
Survivors began looking for lost family members.
Papa! Papa!
Gracie! Thank goodness I've found you.
My husband, I think he was lost in the fire.
Now, now. He may turn up. Everyone seems lost right now.

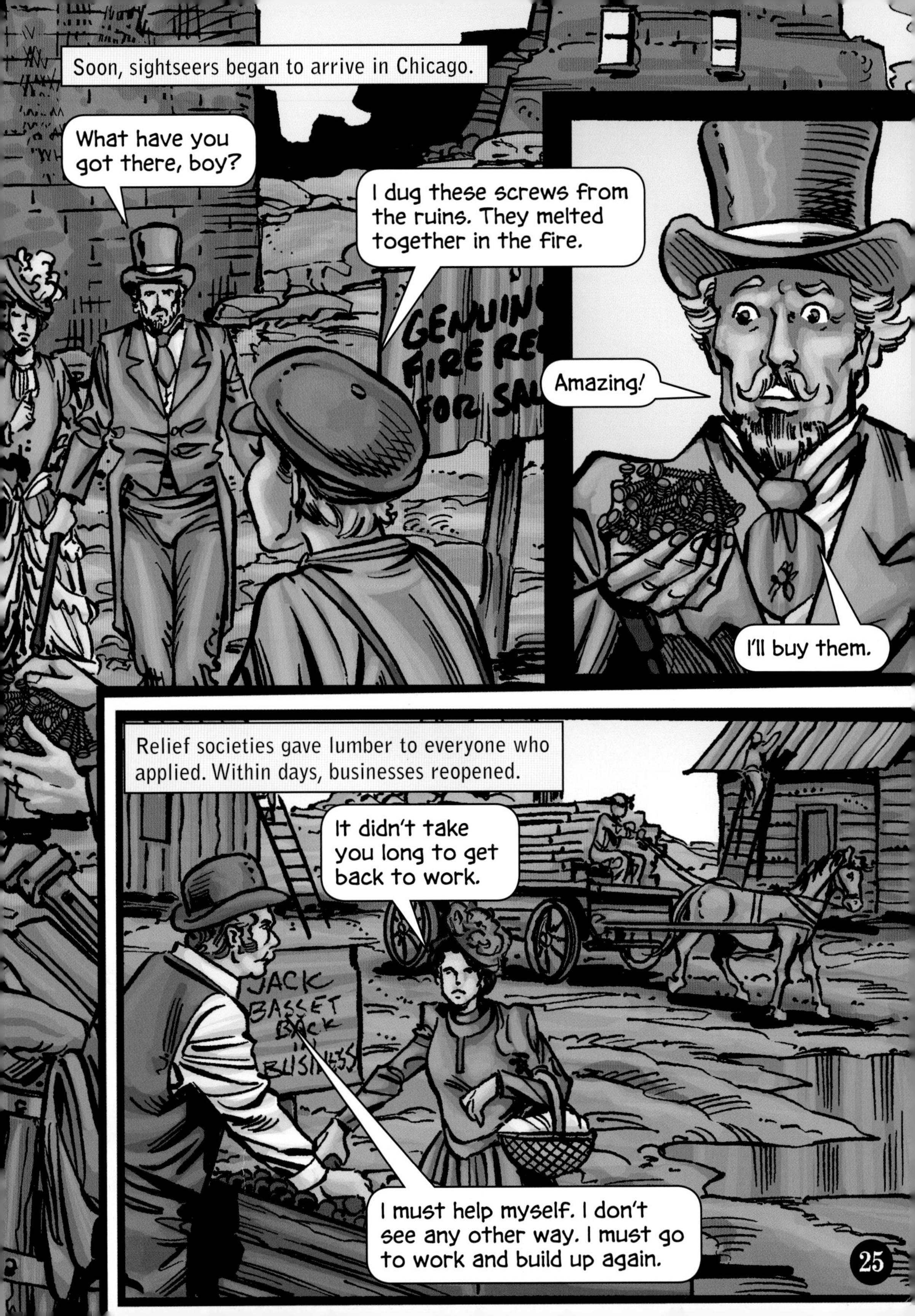
Soon, sightseers began to arrive in Chicago.
What have you got there, boy?
I dug these screws from the ruins. They melted together in the fire.
Amazing!
I'll buy them.
Relief societies gave lumber to everyone who applied. Within days, businesses reopened.
It didn't take you long to get back to work.
JACK BASSET BACK IN BUSINESS
I must help myself. I don't see any other way. I must go to work and build up again.

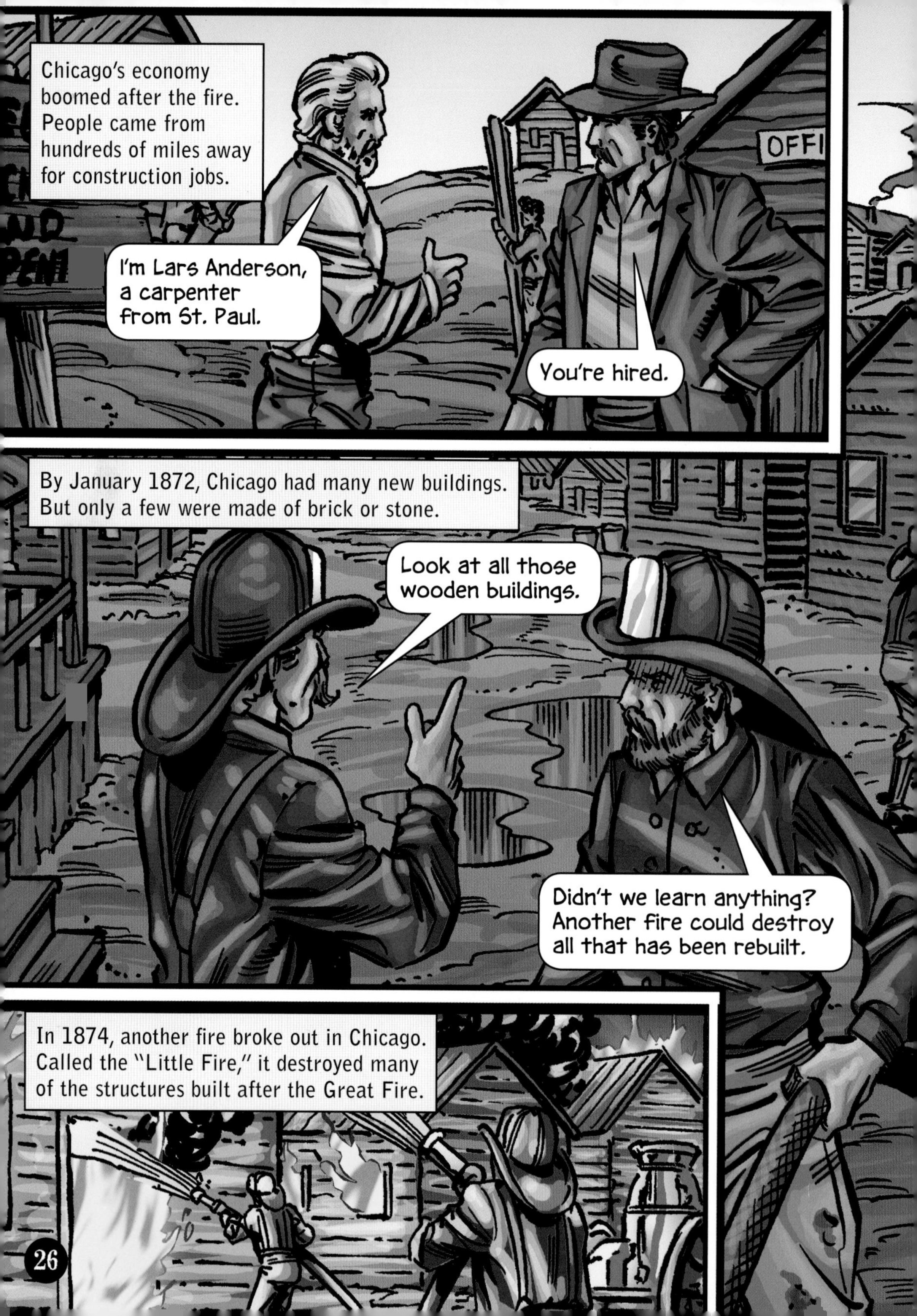
Chicago's economy boomed after the fire. People came from hundreds of miles away for construction jobs.
I'm Lars Anderson, a carpenter from St. Paul.
You're hired.
By January 1872, Chicago had many new buildings. But only a few were made of brick or stone.
Look at all those wooden buildings.
Didn't we learn anything? Another fire could destroy all that has been rebuilt.
In 1874, another fire broke out in Chicago. Called the "Little Fire," it destroyed many of the structures built after the Great Fire.

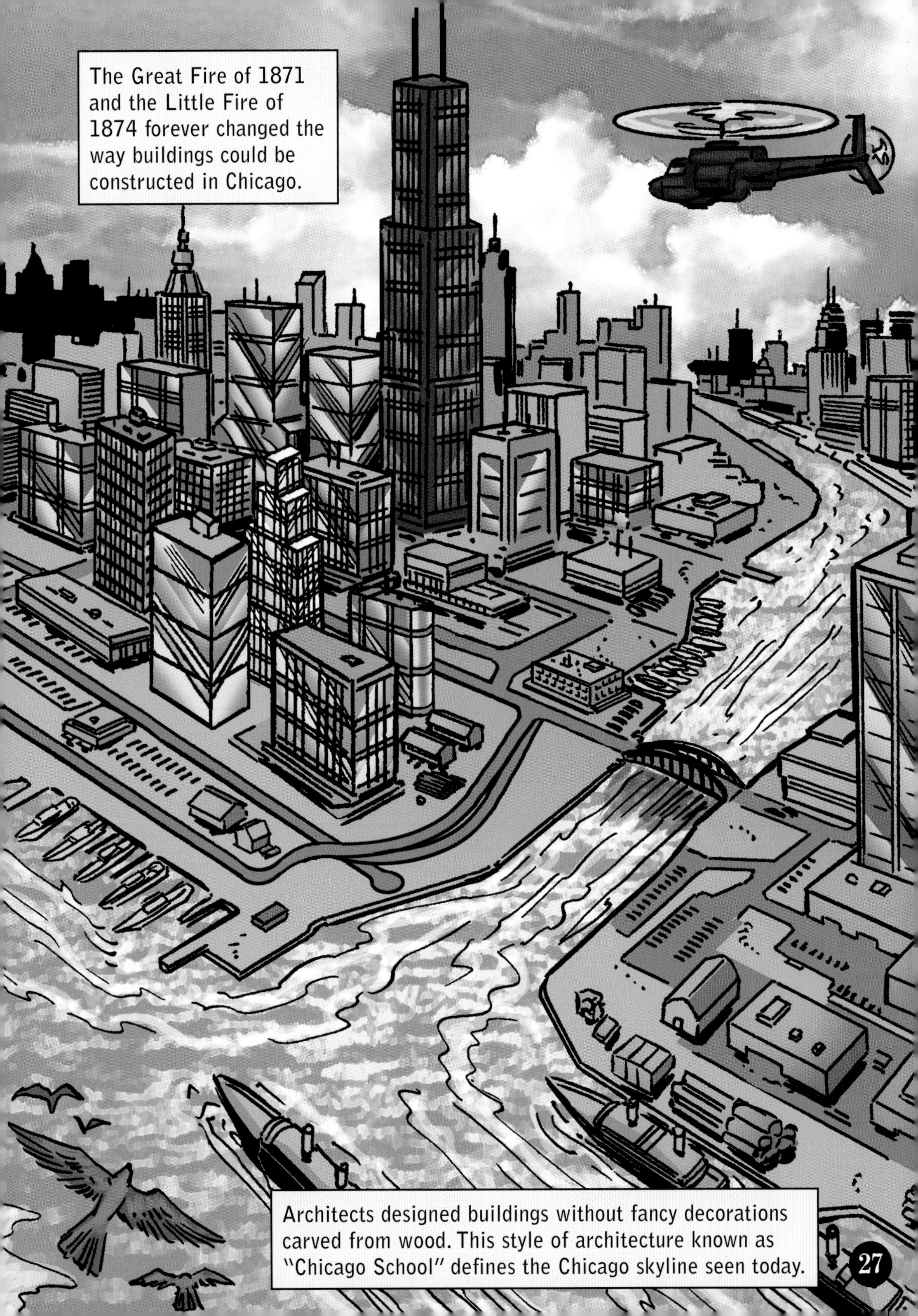
The Great Fire of 1871 and the Little Fire of 1874 forever changed the way buildings could be constructed in Chicago.
Architects designed buildings without fancy decorations carved from wood. This style of architecture known as "Chicago School" defines the Chicago skyline seen today.

MORE ABOUT THE
CHICAGO FIRE

At the time of the Great Fire, Chicago was the fourth largest city in the United States. About 334,000 people lived in the city. The Great Fire killed about 300 people and left another 100,000 homeless. The Great Fire destroyed property valued at $192,000,000.

In 1871, telephones, radios, and televisions did not exist. Most people in Chicago did not know about the fire until they saw the flames or neighbors knocked on their doors. Telegraph messages sent word of Chicago's fire to other cities. Fire engines from nearby towns could not arrive in time to help fight the fire.

How did the Great Fire start? No one is sure, but we do know it started in the O'Leary barn. Many myths and legends suggest Catherine O'Leary's cow kicked over a lantern that started the fire. But Patrick and Catherine O'Leary were in bed when the fire started. Many people unfairly accused the O'Learys of causing Chicago's Great Fire.

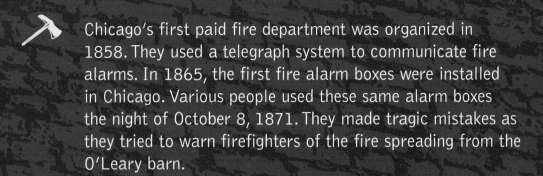 Chicago's first paid fire department was organized in 1858. They used a telegraph system to communicate fire alarms. In 1865, the first fire alarm boxes were installed in Chicago. Various people used these same alarm boxes the night of October 8, 1871. They made tragic mistakes as they tried to warn firefighters of the fire spreading from the O'Leary barn.

How did the fire department make so many mistakes the night of October 8, 1871? Fire alarm boxes were locked to prevent false alarms. No one knows why, but the alarm box at Goll's drugstore never sent the first alarm to the station or to the central fire office. Fire watchers at the courthouse incorrectly guessed the location of the fire in O'Leary's barn. They sounded the wrong alarm box more than once.

Today, Chicago's Fire Department Training Academy sits on the site of the original O'Leary home and barn. Standing at the corner of DeKoven and Jefferson Streets, visitors can view the area where the Great Chicago Fire started in 1871. A point marked on the floor of the academy is said to be the exact spot where the O'Leary barn caught fire.

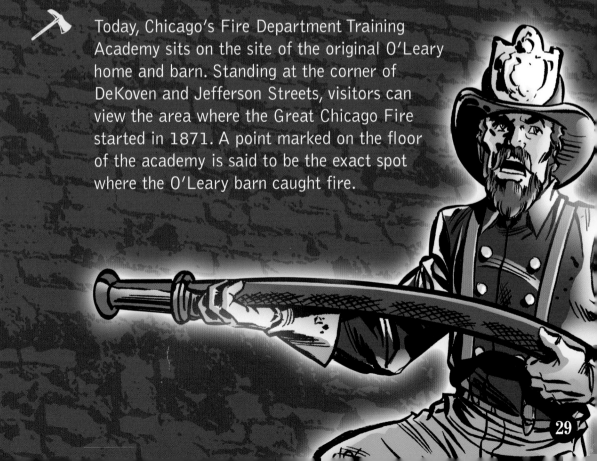

GLOSSARY

fire alarm box (FIRE uh-LARM BOKS)—boxes numbered to show location, placed at different areas throughout the city; a signal from the alarm box sent an alarm to the fire station nearest to the fire.

fire watch office (FIRE WOCH OFF-iss)—a central location in the cupola of the courthouse in 1871 in Chicago; a firewatcher was stationed there at all hours to watch the city for any unreported fires.

tenement (TEH-nuh-muhnt)—a run-down apartment building, especially one that is crowded and in a poor part of a city

waterworks (WAW-tur-wurks)—the system that provides water to a community or town, including reservoirs, pipes, machinery, and buildings

INTERNET SITES

FactHound offers a safe, fun way to find Internet sites related to this book. All of the sites on FactHound have been researched by our staff.

Here's how:

1. *Visit www.facthound.com*
2. Type in this special code **0736854800** for age-appropriate sites. Or enter a search word related to this book for a more general search.
3. Click on the **Fetch It** button.

FactHound will fetch the best sites for you!